FAIRY POEMS

FOR THE VERY YOUNG

Illustrated by

Beverlie Manson

Doubleday & Company, Inc.
Garden City, New York

To Emma, Daniel, and Roger…
who know the way to Fairyland.

Library of Congress Catalog Card Number 80-2758
ISBN: 0-385-17542-6
Copyright © 1982 by Beverlie Manson
All Rights Reserved
Printed in the United States of America

First Edition
Grateful acknowledgment is made to the following for permission to reprint their copyrighted material.

"The Little Elf" by John Kendrick Bangs from the book *A Saint Nicholas Anthology* edited by Burton Frye. Copyright © 1969 by Meredith Press Division, The Meredith Corporation. Reprinted by permission of Hawthorn Properties (Elsevier-Dutton Publishing Company, Inc.).
"Finding Fairies" by Marjorie Barrows, originally appeared in *Child Life Magazine.* Copyright 1923, 1951 by Rand McNally & Company. Reprinted by permission of the author.
"Around a Toadstool Table" from *Songs from Around a Toadstool Table* by Rowena Bastin Bennett. Copyright 1930 by Follett Publishing Company. Used by permission of Follett Publishing Company.
"Fairies" from *Rhymes about Ourselves* by Marchette Chute. Copyright 1932 (Macmillan), renewal © 1960 by Marchette Chute. Reprinted by permission of the author.
"The Spider's Web" by Charlotte Druitt Cole from *The Merry-Go-Round.*

"Fairy Umbrellas" by Lucy Diamond from *Mrs. Strang's Annual for Children* by Herbert Strang. Reprinted by permission of Oxford University Press.

"A Fairy Song" by Elizabeth Dillingham from *1,000 Poems for Children* selected by Elizabeth Hough Sechrist, 1946 Macrae Smith Company.

"Fairies" from *Eleanor Farjeon's Poems for Children.* Originally published in *Joan's Door* by Eleanor Farjeon: Copyright 1926, 1954 by Eleanor Farjeon. By permission of J. B. Lippincott, Publishers and Harold Ober Associates, Inc.

"Fairy Lore," "Fairy Song," and "I Stood Against the Window" from *The Rose Fyleman Fairy Book* by Rose Fyleman. Copyright 1923 by George H. Doran. Reprinted by permission of Doubleday & Company, Inc. and The Society of Authors as Literary Representative to the Estate of Rose Fyleman.
"Have You Watched the Fairies" and "The Fairies Have Never a Penny to Spend" from *Fairies & Chimneys* by Rose Fyleman. Copyright 1918, 1920 by George H. Doran. Reprinted by permission of Doubleday & Company, Inc. and The Society of Authors as Literary Representative to the Estate of Rose Fyleman.
"Fairy Wings" by Winifred Howard from *Out of the Everywhere.* Reprinted by permission of Oxford University Press.
"Flower-Fairies" by Philip Bourke Marston.

"The Snow" by Nellie Burgett Miller from *Child Life Magazine.* Copyright 1926, 1954 by Rand McNally & Company.
"In the Moonlight" by Norreys Jepson O'Connor.

"Take Care" by Rose Waldo from *Child Life Magazine.* Copyright 1925, 1953 by Rand McNally & Company. Reprinted by permission of Rand McNally & Company.
"Fairies' Light" by Alice Wilkins from THE GOLDEN FLUTE: An Anthology of Poetry for Young Children, selected by Alice Hubbard and Adeline Babbett. Copyright 1932, © 1960 by Harper & Row, Publishers, Inc. A John Day book. By permission of Thomas Y. Crowell, Publishers.
"Once When You Were Walking" from FOR DAYS AND DAYS: A Year-round Treasury of Child Verse by Annette Wynne. Copyright 1919 by Harper & Row, Publishers, Inc. Renewed, with extensions, 1947, by Annette Wynne. By permission of J. B. Lippincott, Publishers.

CONTENTS

FAIRIES

Don't go looking for fairies.
They'll fly away if you do.
You never can see the fairies
Till they come looking for you.

—*Eleanor Farjeon*

from *I STOOD AGAINST THE WINDOW*

I stood against the window
    And looked between the bars,
And there were strings of fairies
    Hanging from the stars;
Everywhere and everywhere
    In shining, swinging chains;
The air was full of shimmering,
    Like sunlight when it rains.

—*Rose Fyleman*

IN THE MOONLIGHT

The Fairies dance the livelong night
Across the moonlit hill;
The moonbeams dance along the lake;
The western wind is still.
The waters make a little sound
More sweet than music far —
Oh let me fly across the world
To where the Fairies are!

—*Norreys Jepson O'Connor*

from TAKE CARE

Be still, Mr. Wind, be still!
For out on the top of the hill,
Where trailing arbutus and bluebells grow
And daisies swing and violets blow,
The fairies have brushed away the snow
   From everything
   And dance and sing
   In merry ring!

— Rose Waldo

from FINDING FAIRIES

When the winds of March are wakening
  The crocuses and crickets,
Did you ever find a fairy near
  Some budding little thickets,
A-straightening her golden wings and
  Combing out her hair?
      She's there!

— Marjorie Barrows

THE SPIDER'S WEB

Spider! Spider!
  What are you spinning?
A cloak for a fairy
  I'm just beginning.

What is it made of,
  Tell me true?
Threads of moonshine
  And pearls of dew.

When will the fairy
  Be wearing it?
Tonight, when the glow-worm
  Lamps are lit.

Can I see her
  If I come peeping?
All good children
  Must be then sleeping.

—Charlotte Druitt Cole

from FLOWER-FAIRIES

Flower Fairies—have you found them,
  When the summer's dusk is falling,
With the glow-worms watching round them;
  Have you heard them softly calling?

—Philip Bourke Marston

12

ONCE WHEN YOU WERE WALKING

Once when you were walking across the
  meadow grass,
A little fairy touched you—but you
  never saw her pass.

One day when you were sitting upon a
  mossy stone,
A fairy sat beside you, but you thought
  you were alone.

So no matter what you do, no matter
  where you go,
A fairy may be near you—but you may
  never know.

—Annette Wynne

from THE FAIRIES HAVE NEVER A PENNY TO SPEND

The fairies have never a penny to spend,
  They haven't a thing put by;
But theirs is the dower of bird and of flower.
  And theirs are the earth and the sky.
And though you should live in a palace of gold
  Or sleep in a dried-up ditch,
You could never be poor as the fairies are,
  Or never as rich.

—Rose Fyleman

AROUND A
TOADSTOOL TABLE

Around a toadstool table
  I dine with fairy kings;
    Across the moon-white hilltops
      I dance in fairy rings;
        And when I sleep, I nestle
          Where fairies fold their wings.

— Rowena Bennett

from FAIRY SONG

Dance, little friend, little friend breeze,
Low among the hedgerows, high among
    the trees;
Fairy partners wait for you, oh, do not miss
    your chance,
      Dance, little friend, dance!

Sing, little friend, little friend stream,
Softly through the mossy nooks where fairies lie
    and dream;
Sweetly by the rushes where fairies sway and
    swing.
      Sing, little friend, sing!

— Rose Fyleman

FAIRY LORE

Fairies learn to dance before they learn
    to walk;
Fairies learn to sing before they learn to
    talk;
Fairies learn their counting from the cuckoo's
    call;
They do not learn Geography at all.

Fairies go a-riding with witches on their brooms
And steal away the rainbows to brighten up
    their rooms;
Fairies like a sky-dance better than a feast;
  They have a birthday once a week at least.

Fairies think the rain as pretty as the sun;
Fairies think that trespass-boards are only made
    for fun;
Fairies think that peppermint's the nicest thing
    they know;
  I *always* take a packet when I go.

                          —*Rose Fyleman*

THE LITTLE ELF

I met a little Elf-man once,
  Down where the lilies blow.
I asked him why he was so small,
  And why he didn't grow.

He slightly frowned, and with his eye
  He looked me through and through.
"I'm quite as big for me," said he,
  "As you are big for you."

—John Kendrick Bangs

CHILDREN, CHILDREN, DON'T FORGET

Children, children, don't forget
There are elves and fairies yet.

Where the knotty hawthorn grows
Look for prints of fairy toes.
Where the grassy rings are green
Moonlight dances shall be seen.
Watch and wait: O lucky you,
If you find a fairy shoe:
For a ransom he will pay,
Hobbling barefoot all the day.
Lay it on his mushroom seat,
Wish your wish, and go your way.
If your wish should be discreet,
Never fear but he will pay.

—Dora Owen

20

FAIRY UMBRELLAS

Out in the waving meadow grass
  The pretty daisies grow,
I love to see their golden eyes,
  Their petals white as snow.

I wonder if the fairies use
  The dainty little flowers,
To keep their frocks from getting wet
  In sudden April showers.

—*Lucy Diamond*

HAVE YOU WATCHED
THE FAIRIES?

Have you watched the fairies when the rain is done
Spreading out their little wings to dry them in the sun?
  I have, I have! Isn't it fun?

Have you heard the fairies all among the limes
Singing little fairy tunes to little fairy rhymes?
  I have, I have, lots and lots of times!

Have you seen the fairies dancing in the air,
And dashing off behind the stars to tidy up their hair?
  I have, I have; I've been there!

—*Rose Fyleman*

A FAIRY VOYAGE

If I were just a fairy small,
  I'd take a leaf and sail away,
I'd sit astride the stem and guide
  It straight to Fairyland and stay.

— Unknown

FAIRIES

You can't see fairies unless you're good,
  That's what Nurse said to me.
They live in the smoke of the chimney,
  Or down in the roots of a tree;
They brush their wings on a tulip,
  Or hide behind a pea.

But you can't see fairies unless you're good,
  So they aren't much use to me.

— Marchette Gaylord Chute

from FAIRY FROLIC

By a silver fountain,
  In a magic hour,
Once I saw a Fairy,
  Lovely as a flower;
Rainbow morning glories
  Watched her from above;
Waterlilies peeped beneath,
  Just to show their love!

—*Annie Rentoul*

from FAIRY WINGS

Through the windmills
Fairies weave
Stuff for wings
From the breath
Of the winds
On the hills.

From the South
Comes the blue;
From the West
Saffron hue;
From the East
Comes the rose,
And the North
Brings the silver
From the snows.

—*Winifred Howard*

from A FAIRY SONG

Buttercups in the sunshine look
   Like little cups of gold.
Perhaps the fairies come to drink
   The raindrops that they hold.

The daisies with their gold hearts
   Fringed all about with white,
Are little plates for fairy folk
   To sup from every night.

—Elizabeth T. Dillingham

FAIRIES' LIGHTS

Fireflies are fairies' lights —
Twink! Blinkety! Wink!

First the fairies turn them on
Then turn them off with
a blink!

The fairies never dance by day
For night is best — they think.
The fireflies turn on and off —
Twink! Blinkety! Wink!

—Alice Wilkins

THE SNOW

The snow's a snuggly blanket
  The fairies tuck around
The sleeping posies in their beds,
  Safe in the crumbly ground.

They cover all so gently
  And softly say, "Good night,"
Then steal away and leave them,
  All snug and warm and white.

—*Nellie Burget Miller*

30